IKARIA DIET COOKBOOK FOR BEGINNERS

Enjoy our easy and simple flavorful 100+ recipes, with delicious tasty 28day meal plan to nourish ikaria beginners for healthy and living longer well-being.

Dr, Mary Tanner

Dr, Mary Tanner

Dr, Mary Tanner

TABLE OF CONTENTS

Dr, Mary Tanner

Dr, Mary Tanner

Day 3:

Day 4:

Day 5:

Day 6:

Day 7:

Day 8:

Day 9:

Day 10:

Day 11:

Day 12:

Day 13:

Day 14:

Day 15:

Day 16:

Day 17:

Day 18:

Day 19:

Day 20:

Day 21:

Day 22:

Day 23:

Day 24:

Day 25:

Day 26:

Dr, Mary Tanner

Dr, Mary Tanner

ABOUT THE AUTHOR

Meet Dr. Mary Tanner, a passionate advocate for healthy living and the author behind the Ikaria Diet Cookbook for Beginners. With her deep knowledge of nutrition and her love for Mediterranean cuisine, Dr. Tanner has crafted a collection of delicious and nourishing recipes inspired by the vibrant flavors of Ikaria. Through her expertise and dedication to promoting wellness, Dr. Tanner invites readers to embrace the Ikarian lifestyle and embark on a journey to better health and vitality. Join her as she shares the secrets of longevity and well-being found in the heart of the

Dr, Mary Tanner

Mediterranean. Welcome to a world of delicious possibilities with Dr. Mary Tanner.

INTRODUCTION

Welcome to the Ikaria Diet Cookbook for Beginners, your passport to the enchanting world of Ikarian cuisine and the secrets of longevity and well-being. Nestled in the azure waters of the Aegean Sea, the island of Ikaria has long been celebrated as a haven of health and vitality, where residents boast

Dr, Mary Tanner

some of the highest life expectancies in the world.

In this delightful cookbook, we invite you to embark on a culinary journey to Ikaria, where the air is scented with the aroma of freshly harvested herbs, and the sun-kissed flavors of the Mediterranean dance on your palate. Whether you're a seasoned chef or a kitchen novice, our cookbook offers a tantalizing array of easy-to-follow recipes that capture the essence of Ikarian cuisine.

From nourishing soups and hearty stews to succulent seafood specialties and indulgent desserts, each dish is crafted with love and care to showcase the bountiful flavors of the

Dr, Mary Tanner

island. Drawing inspiration from the freshest seasonal ingredients and time-honored cooking techniques, our recipes are designed to nourish both body and soul, while delighting your taste buds with every bite.

More than just a collection of recipes, the Ikaria Diet Cookbook for Beginners is a celebration of the Ikarian way of life—a lifestyle rooted in simplicity, community, and connection to the land. As you explore the pages of this book, you'll discover the joy of cooking with fresh, wholesome ingredients, and the profound sense of well-being that comes from sharing delicious meals with loved ones.

Dr, Mary Tanner

So, whether you're seeking to improve your health, boost your energy levels, or simply savor the pleasures of good food, let the Ikaria Diet Cookbook for Beginners be your guide to a happier, healthier, and more vibrant life. Join us on this culinary adventure and discover the magic of Ikarian cuisine. Bon appétit!"

WHAT EXACTLY IS IKARIA DIET?

The typical eating patterns of the people who live on the Greek island of Ikaria in the

Dr, Mary Tanner

Aegean Sea are referred to as the Ikarian diet. Ikaria has drawn notice due to its high percentage of centenarians, or individuals who live to reach 100 years old, and its status as a "Blue Zone," an area where the average person lives longer and in better health than the rest of the world.

The Ikarian diet is similar to the Mediterranean diet in general, but it also has some special components that are particular to the island's produce and culinary customs. Among the essential components of the Ikarian diet are:

Plant-based foods: A diet high in fruits, vegetables, whole grains, and legumes is recommended. Ikarians eat a wide range of seasonal foods, such as herbs, tomatoes, beans, and greens.

Olive oil: Used for both cooking and salad dressing, olive oil is a fundamental fat in the

Dr, Mary Tanner

Ikarian diet. It provides antioxidants and good monounsaturated fats.

Ikarians frequently search for wild greens and herbs, which are then used in a variety of cuisines. These consist of sage, wild spinach, fennel, and dandelion greens.

Fish and seafood: Consuming fish and seafood on a daily basis gives you access to protein and omega-3 fatty acids. Sardines and anchovies are two common tiny, oily fish eaten by Ikarians.

Dairy: Products made from goats or sheep, such as cheese and yogurt, should be consumed in moderation.

Wine: Red wine is typically drunk in moderation in Ikaria and is frequently paired with meals. Small amounts of wine are generally drank, and excessive drinking is not seen as a part of the cultural and social fabric.

Dr, Mary Tanner

Limited meat consumption: Although it's not completely off limits, meat is usually eaten less frequently and in smaller portions than on other diets.

Social and lifestyle factors: In addition to eating habits, the Ikarian lifestyle places a strong emphasis on stress management, exercise, and social interaction—all of which are beneficial to general health and wellbeing.

All things considered, the Ikarian diet places a strong emphasis on complete, minimally processed meals, plant-based ingredients, and a balanced eating style, all of which probably help explain the islanders' long life and good health.

KEY INGREDIENTS AND COOKING TECHNIQUES

Dr, Mary Tanner

The history, customs, and availability of regional foods on the island are all reflected in the Ikarian diet. The following essential components and cooking methods are essential to an Ikarian diet:

Local Produce: A wide range of fruits and vegetables, including tomatoes, cucumbers, peppers, eggplants, zucchinis, and leafy greens like spinach and kale, are produced on Ikaria's lush land. Many Ikarian cuisines start with these seasonal, fresh ingredients.

Wild Greens and Herbs: Ikarians frequently pick wild greens and herbs from the hillsides and surrounding countryside as part of their customary habit of foraging the island. Wild greens that are high in nutrients and flavor, such wild fennel, chicory, and dandelion greens, are highly valued. Herbs such as sage, thyme, and oregano give many meals a fragrant depth.

Dr, Mary Tanner

Olive Oil: An essential part of the Ikarian diet, olive oil is generously used in cooking as well as as a vinaigrette for veggies and salads. Extra virgin olive oil made locally has a strong flavor and is a good source of antioxidants and monounsaturated fats.

Legumes: Three main ingredients in Ikarian cuisine are beans, lentils, and chickpeas. They are frequently used to soups, stews, and salads and are high in protein, fiber, and other minerals.

Whole Grains: On Ikaria, people frequently eat whole grains such barley, bulgur wheat, and whole wheat bread. These grains are frequently served with vegetables, lentils, or seafood and offer long-lasting energy.

Fresh seafood is readily available in Ikaria due to its island location. Sardines, anchovies, and mackerel are typical examples of small, oily fish that are high in

Dr, Mary Tanner

protein, omega-3 fatty acids, and other vital elements.

Dairy Products: Ikarian cuisine emphasizes moderation in the consumption of dairy products such yogurt, cheese, and milk. Products made from the milk of goats and sheep are especially popular and are used in both savory and sweet recipes.

Wine: A staple of Ikarian culture, wine is typically savored sparingly, particularly during meals. Red and white wines from the area enhance the flavors of the cuisine and are a great addition to parties and festivities.

Simple Cooking Methods: Ikarian cooking is characterized by the use of straightforward, rustic methods that highlight the flavors of the food. Grilling, roasting, stewing, and sautéing are common culinary techniques that frequently involve the use of aromatic herbs and olive oil.

Dr, Mary Tanner

Social and Cultural Significance: In Ikaria, eating is not only about being nourished, but also about interacting with others and strengthening bonds with loved ones. Getting together at the table to share food, tales, and laughing is a treasured custom that strengthens ties within the community and enhances general wellbeing.

In general, the Ikarian diet emphasizes simple cooking techniques, seasonal, fresh foods, moderation, and social relationships. It also reflects a holistic view to food and life. The Ikaria people's longevity, good health, and overall sense of well-being are all influenced by their eating habits and cultural customs.

KITCHEN ESSENTIALS AND TECHNIQUES

It helps to have certain kitchen necessities and know particular cooking methods in order to prepare Ikarian food well. Key

Dr, Mary Tanner

ingredients and techniques frequently used in Ikarian cookery are listed below:

Essentials for the Kitchen:
Good Olive Oil: Ikarian cooking relies heavily on extra virgin olive oil, which is also used for salad dressing and cooking.

Fresh Herbs: Since these flavor-enhancing herbs are frequently used to season food, stock up on fragrant herbs like oregano, thyme, sage, and rosemary.

Legumes and Grains: For soups, stews, and salads, keep a range of dry beans, lentils, chickpeas, bulgur wheat, and barley on hand.

Local Produce: Seasonal, fresh fruits and vegetables are a common ingredient in Ikarian cuisine. Ensure your pantry is stocked with essentials such as peppers, eggplants, tomatoes, cucumbers, and leafy greens.

Dr, Mary Tanner

fish: For meals high in protein, try to stock your cupboard with fresh or premium canned fish such as sardines, anchovies, mackerel, and octopus.

Greek yogurt and regional cheeses, such as feta or kefalotyri, can be added to recipes to create creamy textures and zesty flavors.

Wine: Having a bottle of good Greek wine on hand can improve the dining experience and be used in some recipes, even if it's not technically necessary for cooking.

Standard Kitchen Utensils: Ikarian cooking requires the use of standard kitchen utensils such as mixing bowls, pots, pans, baking sheets, and knives.

Cooking Methods:
Sautéing and Stir-frying: For soups, stews, and stir-fries, use olive oil to sauté

Dr, Mary Tanner

vegetables, greens, and aromatics like garlic and onions.

Grilling and Roasting: To enhance the flavor of food and bring out the natural essence of vegetables, meats, and seafood, grill or roast them.

Simmering and Stewing: To make filling soups, stews, and casseroles, slowly cook beans, grains, and vegetables in aromatic broths or sauces.

Steaming and Boiling: Use this method to preserve the nutrients and vivid hues of vegetables and grains, which may then be added to salads or served as a side dish.

Marinating: To tenderize and flavor food before cooking, marinate meats, seafood, and vegetables in olive oil, herbs, spices, and citrus juices.

Dr, Mary Tanner

Baking and Braising: For tender, flavorful results, bake or braise meats, fish, and vegetables in the oven with herbs, wine, and other seasonings.

Foraging: To add freshness and flavor to your food, learn how to identify, gather, and cook with wild greens and herbs if you have access to them.

Preserving: To increase the shelf life of seasonal produce and develop distinctive flavors, experiment with traditional preservation methods including pickling, fermenting, and sun-drying.

You'll be ready to make wholesome, flavorful meals at home if you have these staples in your kitchen and can practice these cooking methods.

FRESH SEAFOOD SPECIALTIES

Dr, Mary Tanner

Fresh fish is highly valued in Ikarian cuisine and is frequently served in straightforward yet delectable ways that bring out the inherent flavors of the ingredients. Here are a few instances of popular fresh seafood dishes in Ikaria:

Seafood abounds in the waters surrounding Ikaria, and a common way to savor their rich, oily flavor is to roast them over an open flame. Just toss the sardines with salt, pepper, lemon juice, and olive oil and grill until they are cooked through and beginning to brown.

Octopus in Wine Sauce: Another seafood specialty that's popular in Ikaria is octopus. It can be made softer and more flavorful by cooking it in a solution of wine, olive oil, garlic, and herbs. Serve the warm octopus with lemon juice and a drizzle of extra virgin olive oil.

Dr, Mary Tanner

filled Squid (Kalamari Gemisto): Rice, herbs, onions, tomatoes, and occasionally pine nuts or raisins are usually filled into squid. After being cooked until tender in a flavorful tomato sauce, the stuffed squid is served hot and makes a delightful and filling meal.

Fried Anchovies (Gavros Tiganitos): Fried to a crispy perfection, fried anchovies are a mainstay of Ikarian cuisine. Usually cooked in olive oil till golden brown, they are covered in seasoned flour or breadcrumbs and served hot with lemon wedges.

Ikarians love robust seafood stews and soups that are created with a variety of fresh catch, such as squid, shrimp, mussels, and fish. These meals are frequently cooked with herbs, garlic, onions, tomatoes, and maybe a dash of wine for more flavor depth.

Dr, Mary Tanner

Marinated Mackerel (Lakerda): To give the fish fillets flavor, they are marinated in a concoction of vinegar, garlic, olive oil, and herbs. After that, the marinated mackerel is served cold as a cool meze or appetizer, frequently with crusty bread or olives.

Sea bream and sea bass, for example, are frequently grilled whole or in fillet form and seasoned with a mixture of herbs, garlic, lemon juice, and olive oil. The fish is marinated in an aromatic herb marinade until it is flaky and delicate, and it has a smokey charred flavor.

The wealth of ingredients and simplicity of Ikarian cuisine are reflected in these fresh seafood specialties, which let the sea's inherent flavors show through in every dish.

HEARTY MAIN DISHES

Dr, Mary Tanner

Ikarian food offers a range of filling, tasty, and healthful main courses that frequently use fresh foods including veggies, legumes, healthy grains, and occasionally meat or seafood. Here are a few illustrations of filling main courses that are popular in Ikaria:

Ikarian cuisine is known for its classic Greek bean soup, known as fatalada. Fasolada is a simmering dish that consists of white beans (such cannellini or navy beans), tomatoes, onions, carrots, celery, and herbs. The flavors are developed and the beans become delicate. It's typically served with a slice of crusty bread and a sprinkle of extra virgin olive oil.

Revithada: A filling stew made with chickpeas, revithada is a native of Ikaria. To make chickpeas soft and tasty, they are cooked with onions, garlic, tomatoes, olive oil, and a mixture of aromatic herbs. This

Dr, Mary Tanner

meal gets its distinct smoky flavor by being prepared in a clay pot in a wood-fired oven.

Ikaria is known for its traditional Greek tripe soup, known as patsas, which is particularly popular in the winter. Patsas are made by simmering beef or lamb tripe, garlic, onions, tomatoes, and herbs for several hours until the tripe becomes tender and the flavors combine. It is frequently served hot with a dash of black pepper and a squeeze of lemon juice.

Gemista, literally meaning "stuffed vegetables," is a delicacy that's well-liked in both Ikaria and Greece. Hollowed-out tomatoes, bell peppers, zucchini, or eggplants are filled with a tasty concoction of rice, tomatoes, onions, herbs, and occasionally ground beef. After being cooked until soft, the stuffed veggies can be served warm or at room temperature.

Dr, Mary Tanner

Moussaka: Often eaten as a substantial main course, moussaka is a traditional Greek casserole dish. Baked until brown and bubbly, layers of sliced eggplant, potatoes, and ground meat (often lamb or beef) are covered with a creamy béchamel sauce. This recipe is substantial and hearty, making it ideal for special occasions.

Arakas Latheros: Known as Greek-style peas, arakas latheros is a simple but tasty dish that is popular in Ikaria. Tender and aromatic fresh peas are cooked with onions, garlic, tomatoes, olive oil, and dill. It's frequently served as an appetizer with some crusty bread or as an accompaniment to some grilled fish or meat.

Psarosoupa: Fish of various kinds, potatoes, onions, carrots, celery, tomatoes, olive oil, and herbs are combined to make this filling Greek fish soup. The fish is cooked thoroughly by simmering it in a

Dr, Mary Tanner

fragrant broth, creating a filling and cozy soup that's ideal for cold nights.

With every bite, these substantial main meals provide nourishment and delight, embodying the rustic simplicity and profusion of ingredients characteristic of Ikarian cuisine.

TRADITIONAL BEVERAGES

Ikarian culture places a great value on traditional drinks since they provide a sense of refreshment and frequently showcase the island's rich culinary history. Here are a few instances of customary drinks consumed in Ikaria:

Greek Coffee (Ellinikos Kafés): Greek coffee is served in tiny cups and is made with strong, finely ground coffee in a little pot called a briki. Throughout the day, people frequently enjoy it, particularly after

Dr, Mary Tanner

meals or at social events. Greek coffee is prized for its thick consistency, deep flavor, and occasional taste sweetening.

Herbal Teas: A wide range of aromatic herbs and plants may be found growing in the hilly terrain of Ikaria. Many of these plants are utilized to prepare herbal teas that are said to provide medicinal advantages. Herbal beverages that are popular in Ikaria are mountain tea (made from the dried flowers and leaves of Sideritis plants), chamomile tea, and sage tea.

Greek traditional drink Rakomelo is produced by mixing strong spirit (raki) extracted from grapes or other fruits with honey, cinnamon, and occasionally additional spices. It is particularly well-liked in the winter as a cozy and warming beverage, and it is frequently served heated.

Dr, Mary Tanner

Ouzo: A popular liquor with an anise flavor in Greece, especially in Ikaria, is called ouzo. It is usually served with meze, or appetizers, such as olives, cheese, and cured meats, and is consumed as an apéritif or digestif. When ouzo is combined with water, the anise oils dissolve and cause the drink to appear hazy.

Local Wines: Ikaria has a long tradition of producing wine, much like many other Greek locations. Both locals and visitors like the red and white wines that are produced locally. These wines are frequently served with meals and festivities, adding to the friendly ambiance of Ikarian get-togethers.

Tsipouro: Like Italian grappa, tsipouro is a potent distilled alcohol made from the pomace left over following winemaking. Many Greek regions, including Ikaria, have long enjoyed this traditional beverage, which is typically savored as a digestif following a meal. You can drink tsipouro straight or combined with ice and water.

Dr, Mary Tanner

Fresh Fruit Juice: It's customary to savor freshly squeezed fruit juices in Ikaria due to the island's profusion of fresh fruit, which includes pomegranates, oranges, and lemons. In addition to being delicious, these juices offer a cool way to stay hydrated, particularly in the hot summer months.

These customary drinks are a reflection of Ikaria's rich culinary history and are frequently savored during meals, festivities, and social events, which enhances the island's welcoming atmosphere.

HISTORY AND CULTURAL SIGNIFICANCE

The island's long-standing customs, topography, and way of life are intricately entwined with the historical and cultural significance of Ikarian food. An outline of the background and culture of Ikarian food is provided below:

Dr, Mary Tanner

Historical Context: Ancient Origins: There is evidence of human presence on Ikaria dating back to the Neolithic era, indicating the island's long and rich past. Ikaria has hosted numerous civilizations over the ages, including the Greeks, Romans, Byzantines, and Ottomans, all of whom had an impact on the island's customs and gastronomy.

Greek Influence: Being a part of Greece, Ikaria is connected to the larger Greek culture through numerous cultural and gastronomic traditions. Greek cooking is distinguished by its use of olive oil, herbs, and spices, as well as its emphasis on seasonal, fresh ingredients prepared simply.

Mediterranean Diet: Ikarian food is frequently linked to the Mediterranean diet, which places a focus on whole grains, fruits, vegetables, legumes, nuts, fish, and olive oil while avoiding processed foods and red meat. It is thought that the Mediterranean

Dr, Mary Tanner

cuisine, which is well known for its health advantages, adds to the lifespan and general well-being of Ikarians.

Cultural Significance: Hospitality and Community: Ikarian culture revolves around food, which unites people and promotes hospitality and community. Meals are frequently shared with loved ones, and get-togethers around the table are treasured times for bonding, laughter, and conversation.

Festivities & Celebrations: In Ikaria, food plays a crucial role in these events, with customary foods and specialties being made for important events like marriages, religious holidays, and cultural festivals. Ikarians have the chance to commemorate their customs and cultural history at these occasions.

Nature Connection: Ikarian food has a strong connection to the island's natural

Dr, Mary Tanner

surroundings, as evidenced by the abundance of dishes made with ingredients that are sourced locally, including fruits, wild greens, fresh seafood, and herbs. On the island, gathering wild foods for consumption is a custom that reflects a great reverence for the natural world and its abundance.

Longevity and Health: Ikarian food is well known for its ability to promote health, and many of its traditional ingredients and cooking techniques are linked to long life and good health. Researchers who are interested in learning more about the elements that contribute to the long and healthy lives of Ikarians have taken notice of the island's high rate of centenarians, or individuals who live to reach 100 years old.

In summary, Ikarian food emphasizes seasonal, fresh ingredients, straightforward preparations, and sharing a common love of food, reflecting the island's history, culture,

Dr, Mary Tanner

and natural surroundings. In addition to providing physical sustenance, it also fosters social cohesion, honors Ikaria's rich cultural legacy, and celebrates tradition.

NOURISHING SOUPS AND SALADS

Ikarian cuisine would not be the same without the nourishing soups and salads that showcase the island's seasonal, fresh ingredients while also offering flavor and nourishment. Here are some illustrations of filling salads and soups that are popular in Ikaria:

Soups: Fasolada: Made with white beans (cannellini or navy beans), tomatoes, onions, carrots, celery, and herbs like parsley and oregano, Fasolada is a substantial bean soup. Simmered until the flavors are formed and the beans are soft. A slice of crusty bread and a dab of extra

Dr, Mary Tanner

virgin olive oil are common accompaniments to sosolada.

Revithia: A popular traditional chickpea soup in Ikaria is called revithia. Once soft and tasty, chickpeas are cooked with onions, garlic, tomatoes, olive oil, and herbs. Especially in the winter months, revithia is a warming and filling dish that is frequently served hot.

Avgolemono: Traditionally cooked with chicken broth, eggs, and lemon juice, avagolemono is a traditional Greek soup that is frequently thickened with orzo pasta or rice. This soup is cool and comforting at the same time. It's creamy and tangy. Avgolemono is frequently provided as a healthy and light dinner in Ikaria, especially in the winter.

Salads: Greek salad, or horiatiki salad, is a crisp and vibrant dish composed of tomatoes, cucumbers, red onions, bell

Dr, Mary Tanner

peppers, olives, and feta cheese. It is garnished with dried oregano and drizzled with extra virgin olive oil. It's an essential dish in Greek and Ikarian cooking that highlights the flavors of summer fruit.

Maroulosalata: A light vinaigrette consisting of extra virgin olive oil, lemon juice, salt, and pepper is combined with romaine lettuce, dill, scallions, and occasionally parsley to make this easy salad. This crisp and refreshing salad goes well with a broad range of main courses.

Lahanosalata: Lahanosalata is a thinly sliced cabbage salad with carrots, red onions, and occasionally bell peppers or additional veggies. It's topped with a zesty vinaigrette composed of extra virgin olive oil, mustard, vinegar or lemon juice, and herbs like parsley or dill. Lahanosalata is a year-round dish that is pleasant and hearty.

Dr, Mary Tanner

Beet salad, or panzaria, is prepared by thinly slicing roasted or boiled beets and serving them with fresh herbs like parsley or mint, extra virgin olive oil, vinegar, and/or lemon juice. This colorful and tasty salad goes great with fish or grilled meats.

Ikarian cuisine is known for its filling soups and salads that offer a harmonious blend of tastes, textures, and nutrients, which are a reflection of the island's culinary customs and focus on using seasonal, fresh ingredients.

EMBRACING IKARIAN LIFESTYLE

Taking up the Ikarian way of life involves more than just eating like the people on the island do; it's a whole approach to health that prioritizes relationships with others, exercise, reducing stress, and spending time in nature. The following are some essential

Ikarian lifestyle tenets that you can apply to your own life:

Eat Seasonally and With Mind: Adhere to the Mediterranean diet's tenets, which include an abundance of whole, minimally processed foods such as fruits, vegetables, legumes, nuts, seeds, whole grains, and olive oil. Eat meals carefully, relishing the flavors and textures of your food, and pay attention to portion proportions. Select seasonal, locally sourced ingredients whenever feasible to benefit the environment and your health.

Make Social Connections a Priority: Develop close relationships with your family, friends, and neighbors. Schedule regular get-togethers, meals, and festivities so you may spend time with loved ones and exchange experiences, jokes, and anecdotes. To strengthen your relationships with people, have meaningful conversations and put active listening skills to use.

Dr, Mary Tanner

Keep Yourself Physically Active: Whether it's by dancing, walking, hiking, swimming, gardening, or yoga, make sure you get regular exercise into your daily schedule. For general health and vigor, try to incorporate strength training, flexibility training, and cardiovascular activity. Select pastimes that you find enjoyable and that fulfill you.

Decrease Stress: Make self-care a priority and learn good coping mechanisms. To encourage serenity and mental clarity, engage in relaxation practices like tai chi, deep breathing, mindfulness, or meditation. Take time to relax and enjoy the great outdoors, take up artistic hobbies, or partake in other enjoyable activities.

Establish a relationship with nature by going outside and spending time with it. Enjoy picnics by the shore, go trekking in the mountains, or take leisurely strolls

Dr, Mary Tanner

through parks or wooded regions. By watching the seasons change, gardening, or just taking a moment to sit quietly and take in the beauty around you, you can establish a connection with the cycles of nature.

Develop a Positive Outlook: Encourage an optimistic outlook and develop thankfulness, optimism, and fortitude in the face of adversity. To improve your general well-being, practice mindfulness and keep your attention in the here and now. Be in the company of uplifting people and look for chances to develop yourself and find fulfillment.

Get Enough Sleep: To maintain good physical and mental health, make quality sleep a priority and develop appropriate sleeping habits. To encourage restful sleep, establish a calming bedtime ritual and aim for seven to nine hours of sleep each night. Prior to going to bed, create a peaceful, distraction-free sleeping environment and

Dr, Mary Tanner

stay away from stimulating activities, coffee, and electronics.

You can develop a sense of longevity, vigor, and well-being that embodies the spirit of Ikaria's citizens by adopting the Ikarian way of life and applying these ideas to your day-to-day activities. It's important to keep in mind that developing a holistic approach to happiness and health that feeds your body, mind, and spirit is more important than simply picking up new habits.

GETTING STARTED FOR BEGINNERS

Making tiny, doable changes to your daily routine in order to include healthy behaviors is how beginning adopters of the Ikarian lifestyle get started. Here's a helpful starting guide for beginners:

Discover Ikarian Cuisine and Culture:

Dr, Mary Tanner

Do some research on Ikaria's customs, cuisine, and culture to get a sense of the way of life you want to imitate.

Learn about the essential elements of Ikarian cooking, which include the use of herbs and olive oil, plant-based meals, and fresh, in-season ingredients.

Begin with Minor Dietary Adjustments:

Increase the amount of fruits, vegetables, whole grains, legumes, nuts, seeds, and olive oil in your meals to start.

Try out some easy, tasty, and healthy meals that are influenced by Ikarian cuisine. Go from simple meals like salads, soups, and vegetable-based dishes to more intricate ones.

Make Social Connections a Priority:

Try to make time for friends and family on a regular basis. Arrange get-togethers, dinners, or other occasions where you may spend time with your loved ones.

Dr, Mary Tanner

To build new relationships and widen your social network, get in touch with pals or join neighborhood associations that have similar interests.

Continue to Move:

Make time for physical activity each day, even if it's just a quick stroll or some light stretching.

Discover what kinds of physical activities you prefer doing; it could be yoga, hiking, swimming, or dance.

Use Stress Reduction Techniques:

Include stress-reduction strategies in your everyday routine, such as mindfulness exercises, meditation, or deep breathing exercises.

Determine the sources of stress in your life and investigate constructive coping mechanisms to properly handle them.

Take Time to Enjoy Nature:

Dr, Mary Tanner

Seize the chance to spend time outside, whether it is for gardening, strolling around a local park, or just relaxing in the great outdoors.

Take in the sights, sounds, and fragrances of nature to stimulate your senses, and stop to see the beauty all around you.

Develop a Positive Attitude:

Make an effort to be grateful by thinking back on the things you have each day.

Address pessimistic ideas and foster an optimistic perspective by emphasizing solutions above problems.

Set priorities. Rest:

To tell your body when it's time to wind down, set up a calming nighttime routine and a regular sleep schedule.

Establish a cozy sleeping space that encourages deep, restful sleep, like a calm, dark room with a cozy mattress and pillows.

Seek Assistance and Responsibility:

Dr, Mary Tanner

Tell dependable mentors, family members, or encouraging friends about your ambitions and goals so they can help and inspire you on your path.

For extra motivation and accountability, think about joining online forums or support groups that are centered on health, wellness, or mindfulness.

Keep in mind that changing one's lifestyle is a gradual process, so while you travel this path, have patience and kindness for yourself. No matter how tiny your accomplishments may seem, acknowledge them and keep an open mind to new insights and development.

VEGETARIAN DELIGHTS

Ikarian cuisine, which emphasizes the use of fresh, seasonal vegetables, legumes, grains, herbs, and olive oil, is full of vegetarian delights. Here are some delectable vegetarian recipes that draw inspiration from Ikarian cooking:

Dr, Mary Tanner

Briam: Briam is a typical Greek cuisine that resembles ratatouille. It is prepared with seasonal vegetables such potatoes, onions, zucchini, tomatoes, and bell peppers. Usually, oregano, thyme, and parsley are used to season the veggies, which are then roasted in olive oil until soft and caramelized. This dish is full of flavor and just right for showing the abundance of summer fruit.

Spanakorizo: A tasty and nutrient-dense Greek dish made with spinach and rice. Rice, onions, garlic, tomatoes, dill, and olive oil are cooked together with fresh spinach until the rice is soft and the flavors combine. You can eat this tasty and comforting meal as a side dish or on its own.

Lentil Soup (Fakes): A mainstay of Greek and Ikarian cuisine, fakes is a hearty lentil soup. Once the lentils are soft and the flavors are fully formed, they are cooked with onions, garlic, carrots, celery, tomatoes, olive oil, and herbs. This recipe is filling and healthy, ideal for chilly weather.

Gemista: Gemista, often known as packed veggies, is a well-liked Greek meal that can be had meatless. Hollowed-out tomatoes, bell peppers, zucchini, or eggplants are filled with a tasty concoction of rice, tomatoes, onions, spices, and pine nuts or raisins. After being cooked until soft, the stuffed veggies can be served warm or at room temperature.

Revithia: Revithia is a tasty, hearty, and vegan-friendly traditional Greek chickpea stew. Once soft and creamy, chickpeas are cooked with onions, garlic, tomatoes, olive oil, and herbs. It is frequently served hot with a squeeze of lemon juice and a drizzle of extra virgin olive oil.

Fasolada: A traditional Greek bean soup that is vegetarian-friendly and nutrient-dense. Simmering tomatoes, onions, carrots, celery, and herbs with white beans (such cannellini or navy beans) results in delicate beans with well-developed tastes. This soup is filling and hearty, making it the ideal choice for cold days.

Tzatziki: A cool Greek yogurt dip, tzatziki is made with grated cucumber, garlic, olive oil, lemon juice, and fresh herbs, such as mint or dill. This is a very adaptable condiment that tastes great on salads, pita bread, or grilled veggies.

These tasty vegetarian treats highlight the fresh tastes and healthful ingredients that are essential to Ikarian cooking. These recipes are guaranteed to please your palate and satisfy your body and spirit, regardless of whether you're a vegetarian or just trying to increase the amount of plant-based foods in your diet.

Dr, Mary Tanner

INDULGENT DESSERTS

Even while nutrient-dense, healthful foods are frequently highlighted in Ikarian cuisine, decadent desserts are also savored on special occasions and during celebrations. You can enjoy these delicious pastries while paying homage to the tastes and customs of Ikaria.

Baklava: Layers of flaky phyllo dough, chopped nuts (such pistachios or walnuts), and honey syrup are combined to make this traditional Greek treat. With a pleasing crunch from the nuts and a bit of flowery sweetness from the honey syrup, it's sweet, rich, and incredibly wonderful.

Greek honey puffs known as loukoumades have a crispy outside and a fluffy interior. They are created using a straightforward batter consisting of flour, yeast, water, and a small amount of salt. The batter is then deep-fried till golden brown, after which it is

Dr, Mary Tanner

drizzled with honey syrup and dusted with chopped nuts or cinnamon.

Galaktoboureko: Layers of crispy phyllo pastry and creamy semolina custard combine to make this classic Greek custard pie. After baking until golden, it's covered with a sweet syrup infused with clove, cinnamon, and lemon flavors. It is a really decadent dessert because of the blend of flavors and textures.

Ravani: Soaked in a sweet syrup scented with orange juice and zest, Ravani is a tasty and moist Greek semolina cake. For texture, it's sometimes studded with almonds or walnuts and served with a sprinkling of powdered sugar. If you want to indulge your sweet craving and sample some Ikarian food, Ravani is the place to go.

Greek butter pastries known as koulourakia are typically consumed on celebratory occasions such as Easter. They are produced

Dr, Mary Tanner

from a basic dough that is rolled into different forms and cooked till golden brown. The dough is made using butter, sugar, flour, eggs, and a small amount of brandy or orange juice. Koulourakia are ideal for dipping in coffee or tea since they have a soft texture and are mildly sweetened.

Greek orange phyllo cake, or portokalopita, is a dish that is loaded with citrus flavor. It has layers of buttered phyllo pastry with a semolina custard filling that is seasoned with zest and fresh orange juice. It receives a fragrant and luscious finish from soaking in a sweet syrup flavored with orange blossom water after baking.

Amygdalota: Amygdalota are a type of classic Greek almond cookies that are deliciously sweet and naturally gluten-free. Egg whites, sugar, and ground almonds are combined to make them. The mixture is shaped into little rounds and baked until lightly golden. Amygdalota are frequently consumed as a delicious treat by themselves or with a cup of Greek coffee.

You can indulge your sweet tooth and enjoy the flavors and customs of the Mediterranean while tasting a sample of the sweet side of Ikarian cuisine with these decadent desserts. As part of a healthy lifestyle and balanced diet, enjoy them in moderation.

HEALTHY RECIPES FOR IKARIA BEGINNERS

1. **Ikarian Lentil Soup (Fakes):**
   - Ingredients:
     1. 1 cup brown lentils, rinsed and drained
     2. 1 onion, chopped
     3. 2 carrots, diced
     4. 2 celery stalks, diced
     5. 2 garlic cloves, minced

Dr, Mary Tanner

6. 1 can (14 oz) diced tomatoes
7. 4 cups vegetable broth
8. 1 teaspoon dried oregano
9. 1 bay leaf
10. Salt and pepper to taste
11. Extra virgin olive oil for drizzling
12. Fresh parsley for garnish (optional)

- Instructions:
   1. In a large pot, heat a drizzle of olive oil over medium heat. Add the onion, carrots, and celery, and sauté until softened, about 5 minutes.
   2. Add the minced garlic and cook for another minute until fragrant.
   3. Stir in the lentils, diced tomatoes, vegetable broth, dried oregano, and bay leaf. Bring the soup to a

boil, then reduce the heat and simmer, covered, for about 25-30 minutes, or until the lentils are tender.

4. Season the soup with salt and pepper to taste. Remove the bay leaf before serving.

5. Ladle the soup into bowls, drizzle with extra virgin olive oil, and garnish with fresh parsley if desired. Serve hot with crusty bread for a complete meal.

2. Ikarian Greek Salad:
   - Ingredients:
     1. 2 large tomatoes, chopped
     2. 1 cucumber, chopped
     3. 1 red onion, thinly sliced
     4. 1 green bell pepper, seeded and chopped
     5. 1/2 cup Kalamata olives, pitted
     6. 4 oz feta cheese, crumbled

7. 2 tablespoons extra virgin olive oil
8. 1 tablespoon red wine vinegar
9. 1 teaspoon dried oregano
10. Salt and pepper to taste
- Instructions:
  1. In a large salad bowl, combine the chopped tomatoes, cucumber, red onion, bell pepper, and Kalamata olives.
  2. In a small bowl, whisk together the extra virgin olive oil, red wine vinegar, dried oregano, salt, and pepper to make the dressing.
  3. Pour the dressing over the salad and toss to coat the vegetables evenly.
  4. Sprinkle the crumbled feta cheese on top of the salad

Dr, Mary Tanner

and gently toss again to combine.

5. Serve the Ikarian Greek salad immediately as a refreshing side dish or light lunch.

3. **Ikarian Roasted Vegetables**:
    o Ingredients:
        1. 2 zucchinis, sliced into rounds
        2. 2 bell peppers, seeded and sliced
        3. 1 red onion, sliced
        4. 1 pint cherry tomatoes
        5. 4 garlic cloves, minced
        6. 2 tablespoons extra virgin olive oil
        7. 1 teaspoon dried oregano
        8. Salt and pepper to taste
        9. Fresh parsley for garnish (optional)
    o Instructions:
        1. Preheat the oven to 400°F (200°C). Line a baking

sheet with parchment paper or foil for easy cleanup.

2. In a large bowl, toss together the sliced zucchinis, bell peppers, red onion, cherry tomatoes, and minced garlic.

3. Drizzle the vegetables with extra virgin olive oil and sprinkle with dried oregano, salt, and pepper. Toss until evenly coated.

4. Spread the seasoned vegetables in a single layer on the prepared baking sheet.

5. Roast in the preheated oven for 25-30 minutes, or until the vegetables are tender and slightly caramelized, stirring halfway through cooking.

Dr, Mary Tanner

6. Remove the roasted vegetables from the oven and transfer to a serving dish. Garnish with fresh parsley if desired.
7. Serve the Ikarian roasted vegetables as a flavorful side dish or add them to salads, wraps, or grain bowls for a complete meal.

APPETIZERS RECIPES FOR IKARIA BEGINNERS

1. **Ikarian Dakos (Greek Dakos):**
   - Ingredients:
     1. 4 large whole grain rusks or barley rusks
     2. 2 large tomatoes, diced
     3. 1 cucumber, diced
     4. 1/2 red onion, thinly sliced
     5. 1/2 cup Kalamata olives, pitted and chopped

Dr, Mary Tanner

6. 4 oz feta cheese, crumbled
7. Extra virgin olive oil
8. Dried oregano
9. Salt and pepper to taste
- Instructions:
    1. Place the rusks on a serving platter or individual plates.
    2. In a bowl, combine the diced tomatoes, cucumber, red onion, and Kalamata olives.
    3. Drizzle the vegetable mixture with extra virgin olive oil and season with salt, pepper, and dried oregano to taste. Toss to combine.
    4. Spoon the tomato-cucumber mixture over the rusks, dividing it evenly among them.

Dr, Mary Tanner

5. Top each dakos with crumbled feta cheese and an extra drizzle of olive oil.

6. Serve the Ikarian dakos as a refreshing and flavorful appetizer, perfect for a summer gathering or meal.

2. **Ikarian Tzatziki:**
   - Ingredients:
     1. 1 English cucumber, grated
     2. 1 cup Greek yogurt
     3. 2 cloves garlic, minced
     4. 1 tablespoon extra virgin olive oil
     5. 1 tablespoon fresh lemon juice
     6. 1 tablespoon chopped fresh dill (or mint)
     7. Salt and pepper to taste
   - Instructions:
     1. Place the grated cucumber in a fine-mesh sieve or

cheesecloth and squeeze out excess moisture.

2. In a bowl, combine the strained cucumber, Greek yogurt, minced garlic, olive oil, lemon juice, and chopped fresh dill.

3. Season the tzatziki with salt and pepper to taste and stir to combine.

4. Cover and refrigerate the tzatziki for at least 30 minutes to allow the flavors to meld together.

5. Before serving, taste and adjust the seasoning if necessary.

6. Serve the Ikarian tzatziki as a creamy and tangy dip with pita bread, vegetable crudités, or as a topping for grilled meats or fish.

Dr, Mary Tanner

3. **Ikarian Dolmades (Stuffed Grape Leaves):**
    - Ingredients:
        1. 1 jar grape leaves in brine, drained and rinsed
        2. 1 cup cooked rice (such as Arborio or short-grain rice)
        3. 1/2 cup chopped fresh dill
        4. 1/4 cup chopped fresh mint
        5. 1/4 cup pine nuts, toasted
        6. 1/4 cup raisins, soaked in warm water and drained
        7. 1/4 cup extra virgin olive oil
        8. 1 lemon, juiced
        9. Salt and pepper to taste
    - Instructions:
        1. In a bowl, combine the cooked rice, chopped fresh dill, chopped fresh mint, toasted pine nuts, soaked raisins, extra virgin olive

oil, and lemon juice. Season with salt and pepper to taste and mix well.

2. Place a grape leaf flat on a work surface, shiny side down. Spoon about 1 tablespoon of the rice mixture onto the center of the leaf.

3. Fold the bottom of the leaf over the filling, then fold in the sides, and roll it up tightly into a cylinder shape.

4. Repeat with the remaining grape leaves and rice mixture, making sure to pack the dolmades snugly in the pan.

5. Place the dolmades in a single layer in a large pot or deep skillet. Pour enough water over the

dolmades to cover them, then place a heavy plate or lid on top to keep them submerged.

6. Bring the water to a simmer over medium heat, then reduce the heat to low and cook the dolmades for about 45 minutes, or until the rice is tender.

7. Remove the dolmades from the pot and let them cool slightly before serving.

8. Serve the Ikarian dolmades warm or at room temperature as a delightful appetizer or meze, garnished with lemon wedges if desired.

Dr, Mary Tanner

ENERGIZING BREAKFAST RECIPE FOR IKARIA BEGINNERS

Ikarian Greek Yogurt Parfait with Honey and Walnuts:

- Ingredients:
    1. 1 cup Greek yogurt (preferably full-fat)
    2. 2 tablespoons honey (preferably raw or local)
    3. 1/4 cup walnuts, chopped
    4. 1/4 cup mixed fresh or dried fruits (such as berries, figs, or dates)
    5. Optional toppings: cinnamon, shredded coconut, or granola
- Instructions:
    1. In a serving bowl or glass, layer the Greek yogurt with honey, chopped walnuts, and mixed fruits.
    2. Repeat the layers until you've used up all the ingredients,

ending with a drizzle of honey and a sprinkle of chopped walnuts on top.

3. Optionally, sprinkle some cinnamon, shredded coconut, or granola on top for added flavor and texture.

4. Serve the Ikarian Greek yogurt parfait immediately and enjoy as a delicious and energizing breakfast to start your day on the right foot.

LUNCH RECIPES FOR IKARIA BEGINNERS

Ikarian Chickpea Salad:

- Ingredients:
    1. 1 can (15 oz) chickpeas, drained and rinsed

2. 1 cucumber, diced
3. 1 tomato, diced
4. 1/4 red onion, thinly sliced
5. 1/4 cup Kalamata olives, pitted and halved
6. 2 tablespoons chopped fresh parsley
7. 2 tablespoons extra virgin olive oil
8. 1 tablespoon red wine vinegar
9. Salt and pepper to taste
10. Optional: crumbled feta cheese

- Instructions:
    1. In a large bowl, combine the chickpeas, diced cucumber, diced tomato, sliced red onion, halved Kalamata olives, and chopped fresh parsley.
    2. Drizzle the salad with extra virgin olive oil and red wine vinegar.

Dr, Mary Tanner

3. Season with salt and pepper to taste, and toss gently to combine.
4. If desired, sprinkle crumbled feta cheese on top for added flavor.
5. Serve the Ikarian chickpea salad as a light and refreshing lunch, either on its own or with crusty bread on the side.

Ikarian Lentil and Vegetable Stew:

- Ingredients:
  1. 1 cup brown lentils, rinsed and drained
  2. 1 onion, diced
  3. 2 carrots, diced
  4. 2 celery stalks, diced
  5. 2 garlic cloves, minced
  6. 1 can (14 oz) diced tomatoes
  7. 4 cups vegetable broth

Dr, Mary Tanner

8. 1 teaspoon dried oregano
9. 1 bay leaf
10.   Salt and pepper to taste
11. Extra virgin olive oil
12. Fresh parsley for garnish (optional)

- Instructions:
    1. In a large pot, heat a drizzle of olive oil over medium heat. Add the diced onion, carrots, and celery, and sauté until softened, about 5 minutes.
    2. Add the minced garlic and cook for another minute until fragrant.
    3. Stir in the brown lentils, diced tomatoes, vegetable broth, dried oregano, and bay leaf.
    4. Bring the stew to a boil, then reduce the heat to low and simmer, covered, for about 25-30 minutes, or until the lentils are tender.

Dr, Mary Tanner

5. Season the stew with salt and pepper to taste. Remove the bay leaf before serving.
6. Ladle the Ikarian lentil and vegetable stew into bowls, garnish with fresh parsley if desired, and serve hot with crusty bread or a side salad.

DINNER RECIPES FOR IKARIA BEGINNERS

Ikarian Baked Fish with Lemon and Herbs:

- Ingredients:
    1. 4 fish fillets (such as sea bass, sea bream, or salmon)
    2. 2 lemons, thinly sliced
    3. 4 garlic cloves, minced
    4. 2 tablespoons chopped fresh parsley

Dr, Mary Tanner

5. 2 tablespoons chopped fresh dill
6. 2 tablespoons extra virgin olive oil
7. Salt and pepper to taste

- Instructions:
    1. Preheat the oven to 400°F (200°C). Line a baking dish with parchment paper or aluminum foil for easy cleanup.
    2. Place the fish fillets in the prepared baking dish and season with salt and pepper.
    3. In a small bowl, combine the minced garlic, chopped parsley, chopped dill, and extra virgin olive oil. Mix well.
    4. Spread the herb mixture evenly over the fish fillets.
    5. Arrange the lemon slices on top of the fish.
    6. Bake in the preheated oven for 15-20 minutes, or until the fish is cooked through and flakes easily with a fork.

Dr, Mary Tanner

7. Serve the Ikarian baked fish hot, garnished with additional fresh herbs if desired. Enjoy with a side of roasted vegetables or a simple salad.

Ikarian Greek-Style Beans (Gigantes Plaki):

- Ingredients:
    1. 2 cups dried gigantes (giant white beans) or lima beans, soaked overnight and drained
    2. 1 onion, finely chopped
    3. 2 garlic cloves, minced
    4. 1 can (14 oz) diced tomatoes
    5. 1/4 cup extra virgin olive oil
    6. 2 tablespoons tomato paste
    7. 1 teaspoon dried oregano
    8. 1 teaspoon dried thyme
    9. Salt and pepper to taste

Dr, Mary Tanner

10. Chopped fresh parsley for garnish
- Instructions:
    1. Preheat the oven to 375°F (190°C).
    2. In a large pot, heat the olive oil over medium heat. Add the chopped onion and sauté until softened, about 5 minutes.
    3. Add the minced garlic and cook for another minute until fragrant.
    4. Stir in the soaked and drained gigantes or lima beans, diced tomatoes, tomato paste, dried oregano, dried thyme, salt, and pepper.
    5. Transfer the bean mixture to a baking dish and spread it out evenly.
    6. Cover the baking dish with aluminum foil and bake in the preheated oven for 45-60 minutes, or until the beans are

tender and the sauce has thickened.

7. Remove the foil and bake for an additional 10-15 minutes, or until the top is golden brown and bubbly.

8. Serve the Ikarian Greek-style beans hot, garnished with chopped fresh parsley. Enjoy as a hearty and satisfying main course, accompanied by crusty bread or a side salad.

28DAY MEAL PLAN

Day 1:

- Breakfast: Ikarian Greek Yogurt Parfait with Honey and Walnuts
- Lunch: Ikarian Lentil Soup (Fakes) with a side of Ikarian Greek Salad

Dr, Mary Tanner

- Dinner: Ikarian Baked Fish with Lemon and Herbs served with roasted vegetables

Day 2:

- Breakfast: Whole grain toast with Ikarian Tzatziki and sliced tomatoes
- Lunch: Ikarian Chickpea Salad with crumbled feta cheese
- Dinner: Ikarian Greek-Style Beans (Gigantes Plaki) served with a mixed green salad

Day 3:

- Breakfast: Ikarian Omelette with spinach, tomatoes, and feta cheese
- Lunch: Leftover Ikarian Lentil Soup (Fakes) with a side of whole grain bread

Dr, Mary Tanner

- Dinner: Grilled chicken or tofu marinated in lemon and herbs, served with Ikarian roasted vegetables

Day 4:

- Breakfast: Ikarian Dakos (Greek Dakos) with a side of fresh fruit
- Lunch: Leftover Ikarian Greek-Style Beans (Gigantes Plaki) served with a cucumber and tomato salad
- Dinner: Ikarian Stuffed Bell Peppers with a side of quinoa or brown rice

Day 5:

- Breakfast: Ikarian Green Smoothie made with spinach, banana, Greek yogurt, and honey
- Lunch: Ikarian Lentil and Vegetable Stew with a slice of whole grain bread

Dr, Mary Tanner

- Dinner: Ikarian Grilled Vegetable Platter with hummus and whole grain pita bread

Day 6:

- Breakfast: Ikarian Greek Yogurt with fresh berries and a drizzle of honey
- Lunch: Ikarian Chickpea Salad wrapped in whole grain pita bread
- Dinner: Ikarian Baked Eggplant with tomato sauce and melted feta cheese, served with a side of quinoa or couscous

Day 7:

- Breakfast: Ikarian Frittata with roasted red peppers, onions, and goat cheese

Dr, Mary Tanner

- Lunch: Leftover Ikarian Greek-Style Beans (Gigantes Plaki) served with a mixed green salad
- Dinner: Ikarian Vegetable Stir-Fry with tofu or shrimp, served over brown rice

Day 8:

- Breakfast: Ikarian Greek Yogurt Parfait with Honey and Walnuts
- Lunch: Ikarian Lentil Soup (Fakes) with a side of Ikarian Greek Salad
- Dinner: Grilled Mediterranean Vegetable Platter with hummus and whole grain pita bread

Day 9:

- Breakfast: Ikarian Omelette with spinach, tomatoes, and feta cheese

Dr, Mary Tanner

- Lunch: Leftover Ikarian Greek-Style Beans (Gigantes Plaki) served with a cucumber and tomato salad
- Dinner: Ikarian Baked Fish with Lemon and Herbs served with roasted vegetables

Day 10:

- Breakfast: Ikarian Dakos (Greek Dakos) with a side of fresh fruit
- Lunch: Ikarian Chickpea Salad with crumbled feta cheese
- Dinner: Ikarian Stuffed Bell Peppers with a side of quinoa or brown rice

Day 11:

- Breakfast: Ikarian Green Smoothie made with spinach, banana, Greek yogurt, and honey

Dr, Mary Tanner

- Lunch: Ikarian Lentil and Vegetable Stew with a slice of whole grain bread
- Dinner: Ikarian Grilled Chicken or Tofu Skewers with Mediterranean Couscous Salad

Day 12:

- Breakfast: Ikarian Greek Yogurt with fresh berries and a drizzle of honey
- Lunch: Ikarian Chickpea Salad wrapped in whole grain pita bread
- Dinner: Ikarian Baked Eggplant with tomato sauce and melted feta cheese, served with a side of quinoa or couscous

Dr, Mary Tanner

Day 13:

- Breakfast: Ikarian Frittata with roasted red peppers, onions, and goat cheese
- Lunch: Leftover Ikarian Greek-Style Beans (Gigantes Plaki) served with a mixed green salad
- Dinner: Ikarian Vegetable Stir-Fry with tofu or shrimp, served over brown rice

Day 14:

- Breakfast: Ikarian Greek Yogurt Parfait with Honey and Walnuts
- Lunch: Ikarian Lentil Soup (Fakes) with a side of Ikarian Greek Salad
- Dinner: Grilled Mediterranean Vegetable Platter with hummus and whole grain pita bread

Dr, Mary Tanner

Day 15:

- Breakfast: Ikarian Greek Yogurt Parfait with Honey and Walnuts
- Lunch: Ikarian Lentil Soup (Fakes) with a side of Ikarian Greek Salad
- Dinner: Grilled Mediterranean Vegetable Platter with hummus and whole grain pita bread

Day 16:

- Breakfast: Ikarian Omelette with spinach, tomatoes, and feta cheese
- Lunch: Leftover Ikarian Greek-Style Beans (Gigantes Plaki) served with a cucumber and tomato salad
- Dinner: Ikarian Baked Fish with Lemon and Herbs served with roasted vegetables

Dr, Mary Tanner

Day 17:

- Breakfast: Ikarian Dakos (Greek Dakos) with a side of fresh fruit
- Lunch: Ikarian Chickpea Salad with crumbled feta cheese
- Dinner: Ikarian Stuffed Bell Peppers with a side of quinoa or brown rice

Day 18:

- Breakfast: Ikarian Green Smoothie made with spinach, banana, Greek yogurt, and honey
- Lunch: Ikarian Lentil and Vegetable Stew with a slice of whole grain bread
- Dinner: Ikarian Grilled Chicken or Tofu Skewers with Mediterranean Couscous Salad

Dr, Mary Tanner

Day 19:

- Breakfast: Ikarian Greek Yogurt with fresh berries and a drizzle of honey
- Lunch: Ikarian Chickpea Salad wrapped in whole grain pita bread
- Dinner: Ikarian Baked Eggplant with tomato sauce and melted feta cheese, served with a side of quinoa or couscous

Day 20:

- Breakfast: Ikarian Frittata with roasted red peppers, onions, and goat cheese
- Lunch: Leftover Ikarian Greek-Style Beans (Gigantes Plaki) served with a mixed green salad

Dr, Mary Tanner

- Dinner: Ikarian Vegetable Stir-Fry with tofu or shrimp, served over brown rice

Day 21:

- Breakfast: Ikarian Greek Yogurt Parfait with Honey and Walnuts
- Lunch: Ikarian Lentil Soup (Fakes) with a side of Ikarian Greek Salad
- Dinner: Grilled Mediterranean Vegetable Platter with hummus and whole grain pita bread

Day 22:

- Breakfast: Ikarian Greek Yogurt Parfait with Honey and Walnuts
- Lunch: Ikarian Lentil Soup (Fakes) with a side of Ikarian Greek Salad

Dr, Mary Tanner

- Dinner: Grilled Mediterranean Vegetable Platter with hummus and whole grain pita bread

Day 23:

- Breakfast: Ikarian Omelette with spinach, tomatoes, and feta cheese
- Lunch: Leftover Ikarian Greek-Style Beans (Gigantes Plaki) served with a cucumber and tomato salad
- Dinner: Ikarian Baked Fish with Lemon and Herbs served with roasted vegetables

Day 24:

- Breakfast: Ikarian Dakos (Greek Dakos) with a side of fresh fruit
- Lunch: Ikarian Chickpea Salad with crumbled feta cheese

Dr, Mary Tanner

- Dinner: Ikarian Stuffed Bell Peppers with a side of quinoa or brown rice

Day 25:

- Breakfast: Ikarian Green Smoothie made with spinach, banana, Greek yogurt, and honey
- Lunch: Ikarian Lentil and Vegetable Stew with a slice of whole grain bread
- Dinner: Ikarian Grilled Chicken or Tofu Skewers with Mediterranean Couscous Salad

Day 26:

- Breakfast: Ikarian Greek Yogurt with fresh berries and a drizzle of honey
- Lunch: Ikarian Chickpea Salad wrapped in whole grain pita bread

Dr, Mary Tanner

- Dinner: Ikarian Baked Eggplant with tomato sauce and melted feta cheese, served with a side of quinoa or couscous

Day 27:

- Breakfast: Ikarian Frittata with roasted red peppers, onions, and goat cheese
- Lunch: Leftover Ikarian Greek-Style Beans (Gigantes Plaki) served with a mixed green salad
- Dinner: Ikarian Vegetable Stir-Fry with tofu or shrimp, served over brown rice

Day 28:

- Breakfast: Ikarian Greek Yogurt Parfait with Honey and Walnuts

Dr, Mary Tanner

- Lunch: Ikarian Lentil Soup (Fakes) with a side of Ikarian Greek Salad
- Dinner: Grilled Mediterranean Vegetable Platter with hummus and whole grain pita bread

CONCLUSION

"Embark on a culinary journey to the beautiful island of Ikaria with our Ikaria Diet Cookbook for Beginners. Discover the secrets of longevity and vitality as you delve into the wholesome and flavorful recipes inspired by the Mediterranean lifestyle.

In this cookbook, beginners will find a treasure trove of delicious dishes that celebrate the abundance of fresh fruits, vegetables, legumes, whole grains, and olive

Dr, Mary Tanner

oil—the cornerstones of Ikarian cuisine. From nourishing soups and hearty main dishes to indulgent desserts and traditional beverages, each recipe is thoughtfully crafted to showcase the vibrant flavors and healthful ingredients that define the Ikarian way of eating.

Whether you're seeking to adopt a healthier diet, explore new culinary traditions, or simply savor the joys of good food, our Ikaria Diet Cookbook for Beginners offers something for everyone. With easy-to-follow recipes, helpful tips, and a dash of Mediterranean flair, this cookbook invites you to embrace the Ikarian lifestyle and nourish your body, mind, and soul.

Dr, Mary Tanner

Join us on this gastronomic adventure and discover the art of living well, Ikarian-style. Let the Ikaria Diet Cookbook for Beginners be your guide to a lifetime of delicious meals, vibrant health, and boundless vitality. Cheers to good health and happy cooking!"

THE END

Dr, Mary Tanner

Manufactured by Amazon.ca
Acheson, AB

12897393R00052